How you determine success of training by using an effective evaluation

Trainer's Guide to Evaluation of Training

An Essential Book for Each Trainer

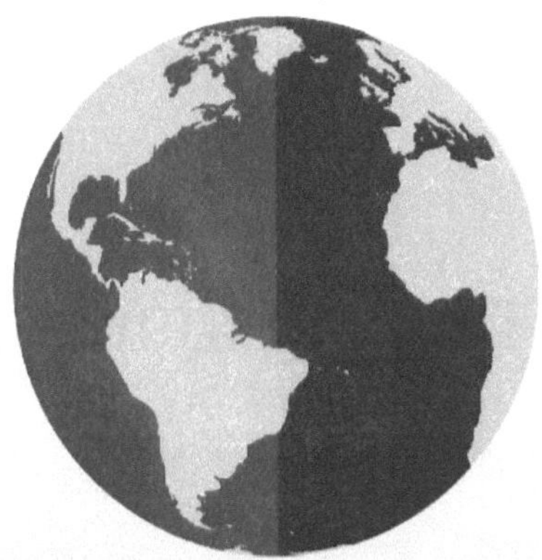

Dr. Lalit Kumar Setia

TRAINER'S GUIDE TO EVALUATION OF TRAINING

An Essential Book for Each Trainer

By

Dr. Lalit Kumar Setia

I S B N – 9781730735325
First Edition - 2018

TABLE OF CONTENTS

TERMS AND ABBREVIATIONS

Sr. No.	Abbreviation	Term
1.	ATI	Administrative Training Institute
2.	CD	Course Director
3.	CDR	Course Director Report
4.	DDOs	Drawing and Disbursing Officers
5.	DDTM	Duties of DDOs in Taxation Matters
6.	DG	Director General
7.	DHE	Department of Higher Education
8.	DoPT	Department of Personnel and Training

9.	DoT	Design of Training
10.	e–TDS	Electronic Tax Deduction at Source
11.	EoT	Evaluation of Training
12.	GST	Goods and Services Tax
13.	IRQ	Immediate Response Questionnaire
14.	MCQs	Multiple Choice Questions
15.	SAT	Systematic Approach to Training
16.	SWOT	Strength, Weakness, Opportunities, and Threats
17.	TDS	Tax Deduction at Source
18.	TNA	Training Needs Analysis

SUMMARY OF RECOMMENDATIONS

The book recommends the following initiatives to improve the effectiveness and efficiency of EoT function on the basis of existing evaluation of training at an institute:

1.	**Preparing and Using Immediate Response Questionnaires (IRQs):** It is required to develop IRQs on which basis the initial and ending behavior can be recorded in terms of their reactions with regard to key training inputs. The IRQs can be analyzed by the training institute for internal validation purposes and by the concerned client organizations and funding agencies for external validation purposes.
2.	**Individual Interviews:** The individual interviews should be used as a tool to record their level of knowledge and skills three times i.e. at starting of the course, mid of the course, and at end of the course for analyzing their learning.

3.	**Preparing and Using Objective Type Tests:** In order to measure the learning outcomes, an objective test should be developed at the end of the course to check and verify the learning of the participants. The objective type test may also include the multiple choice items presenting the practical problems at workspace with the several alternatives to the solutions. The participant may be asked to select the most appropriate solution. The records relating to responses of the participants, on objective tests, should be maintained in the final report of the course.
4.	**Constructing Questionnaires for each course:** For each course, questionnaires are required to be prepared by the subject experts. For example, in case of DDTM Course, a questionnaire comprises exercises to compute the accurate amount of tax deduction at source (TDS) as per rules of income tax act; should be prepared. In order to check the learning of the training session on income tax, the above multi-choice item can be used to test the participants. The records relating to responses of the participants, on questionnaires should be maintained in the final report of the course.
5.	**Role Play Exercises:** The behaviour of the participants should be improved through role play exercises, wherever required. For example, in case of DDTM course, in order to check the learning on provisions of Goods and Service Tax and assess the behaviour of each participant towards implementation of GST, a role play exercise should be developed which may be performed on the 2nd

	day of the course.
6.	**Simulation and In-Tray Exercises:** It is required to frame various simulation and in-tray exercises keeping in view the situations of concerned client organizations. For example, in case of DDTM course, simulation and in-tray exercises should be framed comprising the tasks of ensuring compliance of income tax rules at the workspace.
7.	**Allocation of relevant work to the participants:** In order to check the job performance, the client organization should allocate the similar work to the participants who have undergone the training course so that the learning from the course can be checked and enriched with practical experiences. On the basis of their job performance, the client organization should update the maintained learning logs and send a copy of the same to the training organization and funding agencies so that the next training course may be planned keeping in view the new needs of the participants.
8.	**Measurement of achievement of the key results:** The courses are organized with specific objectives and the evaluation of training also comprises the assessment of achievement of the key results from the course. The training organization, client organization, and funding agencies should check and record the key results achieved in concerned records. It is also required to update the learning logs of the participants accordingly. For example, in case of DDTM course, whether the results have been achieved in the form of

	their enriched learning in this regard that should be checked by DHE and record in the learning logs of the participants with a copy to the training institute and sponsoring authority i.e. DoPT.
9.	**Provision of behavior analysis:** The provision should be made to assess the behavior of the participants during the training and it is required to analysis the same in terms of knowledge, skills, and attitude of the participants. For example, in case of DDTM course, the key stakeholders i.e. DDOs, Director General of Training Institute, Director General of DHE, and Head of DoPT will be provided adequate information to evaluate the effectiveness and efficiency of DDTM course in improving the behavior of the DDOs. On the basis of information of the course, the learning logs of the DDOs will be maintained at both organizations i.e. Training Institute and DHE. On the basis of job performance of DDOs and achievement of key objectives of the training, further training needs will be identified by Training Institution and DHE.
10.	**Maintenance of Learning Logs:** The learning logs should be assessed by the Course Director at the end of the course and include it into the Course Director's report, to keep in the training records of training organization with a copy to the client organization and funding agencies.

11.	**Development of Short Answer Items:** It is recommended to develop short answer items related to components of each course being organized at training institute. For example, in case of DDTM course, the short answer items can be developed by the trainer or guest faculty invited to deliver sessions on income tax. The short answer items can be used every time in DDTM course.
12.	**Preparing Group Exercises for each course:** In order to analyze the behavior of participants, groups should be constituted in each course being organized at an institution. The participants behave differently while working in the constituted groups. The course director and faculties should analyze the behavior of each participant during the course at the time of group interactions. For example, in case of DDTM course, it is must to sharpen social skills of the participants. The participants should be provided group exercises including role-play i.e. roles of DDO, employee, and observer. The DDO should be provided task to deduct accurate amount of tax while the employee should be provided task to convince DDO not to deduct accurate amount of tax due to his weak financial situation. The observer should note down the behavior of both in terms of proposing, giving information, supporting, building, seeking information, summarizing, disagreeing, bringing in, shutting out, defending, and testing. The behavior in the constituted group should be analyzed and noted down by the observer. The

	training organization should utilize the behavior analysis on the basis of role-play exercises and the involvement of the participants to decide their behavior in the situations relating to taxation matters.
13.	**Use and maintain EoT Matrix:** On the basis of active participation of the participant (which may be determined on the basis of IRQs), the job performance should be checked by the client organization. After such analysis, the learning should be recorded in learning logs. On the basis of information, the EoT Matrix can be prepared for both the course as well as participant's learning. For example, in case of DDTM course, the learning should be checked with regard during the course. Further, the information upon the job performance checked by DHE, should be disseminated to the training institution and DoPT. On the basis of information received from participants (in form of IRQs), from training institution (in form of Course Director's Report & comments of Director General, Head of Institution), from DHE (in form of job performance of each participant); the EoT Matrix should be developed by the training organization, DHE, and DoPT for each participant to decide further their training needs. The process of EoT matrix should be used to determine and raise the level of performance of the participants.

INTRODUCTION

The training institutions are established either by Government and Entrepreneurs including private organizations. The organizations are funded by the promotors and investors. A training institution provides training either to the government employees or executives of private organizations. It employs a team of trainers, usually designated as 'Course Directors' in various disciplines like Public Administration, Disaster Management, Financial Management, Behavioral Sciences, Rural Development, Computer Sciences, Sociology, Economic Development etc. A training organization undertakes the work of evaluating each course very seriously. The Head of organization i.e. Director General, himself maintain an excel spreadsheet to evaluate the performance of training inputs and non-training interventions, by manipulating a software in Excel and framing a database by recording the responses of the participants of each course. The responses are analyzed using measures of central tendency, measures of variations, and cross tabulation analysis of the data. Keeping in view, the existing system of evaluating training at an institution, it is required to complete this EoT project for improving the effectiveness and efficiency of the courses organized at training organizations. For this purpose, a course has been selected to be analyzed in terms of EoT function at the training institute i.e. a course organized in July month, sponsored by Department of Personnel and Training (DoPT). The title of the course opted for this purpose was, "Duties of DDOs in Taxation Matters (DDTM).

ACKNOWLEDGEMENTS

The completion of EoT function and formulation of the same in shape of a book, would have been not possible if not dependent on the steadfast support and encouragement of Recognized Trainer Sh. Gaur Hari Khanra. He hence paid equal contribution to the study for which I always feel profound gratitude in my heart.

I would like to express here the very thanks to my boss and advisor, Dr. G. Prasanna Kumar, IAS, Director General, Haryana Institute of Public Administration (HIPA) who provided me the opportunity to do the EoT course and prepare the project report followed by book. I would also like to express my thanks to Sh. M.D. Sinha, Additional Director, HIPA who ushered me in completing the EoT project report within the stipulated time.

I also owe my special thanks to Smt. Neeraja Malik, working as Chief Faculty Training Coordinator (CFTC) & Smt. Ekta Chopra, working as Joint Director at HIPA for sharing his experimental experiences at the time of preparing this EoT report. I also owe my special thanks to Smt. Rekha Dahiya for efforts to stay active in the preparation of EoT report and book by providing necessary support at HIPA.

Nobody has been more important to me in the pursuit of this project than my parents, whose love and guidance are with me whatever I pursue. They are the ultimate role models. Most importantly, I wish to thank my loving and supporting wife, Rashmi, and my daughter, Sanvi, who provide unending inspiration.

EVALUATION OF TRAINING

Project Title

Evaluation of training for a course on **"Duties of DDOs in Taxation Matters"**

About Training Organization

The training organization where the above state course is organized, is a government organization. The organization has the functions of providing training, research and consultancy to improve efficiency and effectiveness in administrative and other functions. The organization endeavors to realize its objectives by enhancing professional knowledge, skills and inculcating attitude necessary for better performance of an individual and also of an organization. Likewise, there are millions of training organizations known for undertaking training and development function. The employees, executives through their heads approach training organizations for undertaking induction and in-service training, executive development programmes (EDPs), faculty development programmes (FDPs), and other events to fill the gap of knowledge, skills, and attitude. The governments, private organizations, world bank, IMF and other sponsoring organizations provide various types of grants and fund to afford such training courses and perform training and development activities.

Apart from grants and funds, the training organizations also earn handsome income from training fees, accommodation facilities, revenue from advertising agencies, and other incomes. The course DDTM was sponsored by Department of Personnel and Training (DoPT), Government of India. The training organization employs a team of trainers, designated as 'Course Directors' in various disciplines like Public Administration, Disaster Management, Financial Management, Behavioral Sciences, Rural Development, Computer Sciences, Sociology, Economic Development etc. The Course Directors have experience of organizing courses on the basis of training needs of the client organizations and they also deliver training sessions.

Existing System of Evaluation in Training Institution

For each course organized at a training institution, various parameters of training's progress and non-training interventions' performance are assessed. The training institution undertakes the work of evaluating each course very seriously. The head of organization i.e. Director General or Principal or Secretary, usually maintains an excel spreadsheet to evaluate the performance of training inputs and non-training interventions, by manipulating a software in MS-Excel and framing a database by recording the responses of the participants of each course. The responses are analyzed using measures of central tendency, measures of variations, and cross tabulation analysis of the data. On the basis of analysis, it is determined to take necessary corrective measures for improving the effectiveness and efficiency of the training function. For this EoT project, a course of DDTM is opted to explain the system of evaluation at the training organization. The course was firstly inaugurated by the Director General on the first day (in first session). Thereafter, the Course Director assessed the initial reactions and expectations of the participants. The participants were asked to explain their expectations from the course so that the course design may be modified (if required). In the course DDTM, after getting the initial reactions and responses with regard to the expectations from the course, various exercises on Goods and Service Tax (GST) had been added containing understanding of practical issues.

About Client Organization of DDTM Course

The client organization is an organization for which a training course is organized. For the course under consideration i.e. DDTM, the client organization is Department of Higher Education (DHE).

The college principals working under Director General, DHE; require to ensure compliance of provisions relating to taxation (including income tax and goods & services tax) in the transactions of colleges. The income tax department also issued guidelines and directions for deducting accurate amount of tax at the time of making payments of salaries and other benefits to the employees, contactors, and other service providers. The college principals are designated as Drawing and Disbursing Officer (DDO) for making financial transactions and ensuring compliance of financial rules including taxation in the colleges.

Performance Problem in DDTM Course

The DDOs working at colleges under Department of Higher Education, lack in knowledge and skills regarding implementing taxation provisions including income tax and goods and services tax.

Training Needs Analysis for DDTM Course in DHE

The need is "To enhance knowledge and sharpen the skills of Drawing and Disbursing Officers (DDOs) for ensuring compliance of taxation provisions in disbursements at their workspace". The Income Tax Department and Excise & Taxation Department have directed the DDOs to ensure deduction of income tax and payment of GST in the financial transactions. As per directions, the DDOs are required to deduct accurate amount of tax known as tax deduction at source (TDS) and also ensure registration of contractors and vendors under Good and Service Tax before having transactions with them. Since every college principal is also designated as Drawing and Disbursing Officer (DDO), need to train for being equipped with knowledge and skills to undertake the activities related to taxation. Lack of such knowledge and skills is a barrier in implementation of taxation provisions in client organization i.e. Department of Higher Education.

About the Course on Duties of DDOs in Taxation Matters (DDTM)

The DDOs are responsible to compliance the provisions of income tax, value added tax, goods and services tax, apart from their duties with regard to drawing and disburse accurate amount in making expenditures at their workplace. Due to large involvement in administrative functions, they suffered from lack of time to deal the work of DDO. Due to their ineffectiveness in compliance of taxation rules, huge loss is born by Government in terms of irregularities and tax evasion. The contractors dealing with DDOs to serve their offices provide their services at cheaper rates by evading the taxes. The employees due to their relationships expect less deduction of tax at source and use false documents or proofs to evade tax in house rent allowance and other allowances. Even deductions u/s 80C to 80U are sometimes misused for tax evasion purposes due to ineffectiveness or involvement of DDOs. The course on "Duties of DDOs in Taxation Matters" sensitizes the DDOs to perform their duties properly by gaining adequate knowledge on the provisions of income tax, goods and service tax, and other issues. The practical exercises and group interactions made them aware of their irregularities at their workplaces and they become more conscious to reduce the irregularities specifically tax evasion by deducting accurate amount of tax deduction at source.

How the course of DDTM be evaluated at the training organization?

Before organizing a course, the training organization undertakes training needs analysis (TNA) of various government organizations on annual basis particularly in December month of each year and on the basis of TNA, training courses are designed and proposed to be organized in upcoming financial year (i.e. April to March). As per the training needs, in each course, aims and objectives are determined in measurable form, "At the end of the course, the participants will be able to ...." For the course of DDTM, the objectives have been stated as under:

By the end of this course participants should be able to:

- Describe the provisions of Income Tax with latest amendments
- Compute Income Tax as per latest amended rules for the Financial Year 2018-19 for ensuring accurate deduction of tax at source
- Submit e-TDS return (24Q) as per Government Instructions
- Describe the provisions of Goods and Services Tax particularly with emphasis upon duties of Drawing and Disbursing Officers (DDOs)

Keeping in view the above stated objectives, the training design is prepared and sent to the DHE. The course has been organized at the training organization and at the end of the quality, quantity; relevance and utility of the training inputs as well as non-training interventions have been evaluated through an evaluation questionnaire provided to the participants for giving their responses on various parameters. At the end of the course, during valedictory address, the participants have also been asked to give their views including remarks on shortcomings of training function, non-training interventions etc.; so that accordingly the improvements can be decided to took place for strengthening the training function of the organization. The evaluation questionnaire used to evaluate the responses of participants of the course "Duties of DDOs in Taxation Matters" is enclosed as Annexure – "A". On the basis of responses of the participants, a Course Director Report (CDR) is prepared by the Course Director and submitted to the Director General of the training organization (enclosed as Annexure – "B"). The CDR with remarks of the Director General is sent to the funding organization i.e. Department of Personnel and Training (DoPT). The information relating to number of participants, their involvement in training, attendance record, and remarks of Course Director; is also sent to the DHE.

Functional Boundaries of the Project

The EoT function can be strengthen for improving the effectiveness and efficiency of the training function of the training organization. At present, the client organizations like DHE are not much aware of contribution of the training organization in developing the human resources and this project focuses on recommending the change in EoT function for prepare and provide information relating to training and development of each participant, on which basis the client organizations can further decide to improve the effectiveness and efficiencies of the employees. It is required to improve the EoT function to have more effective external validation by the client organizations and funding organizations including DoPT. The client organizations and funding organization on the basis of evaluation report will be able to prepare cost-benefit analysis of the course to justify the relevance of training at the training organization.

Why Change? Or Purpose

It is well known, "There is always scope for improvement"; the evaluation of training function at the training organization can further be improved to a great extent by incorporating more techniques of evaluating the training, for improving the effectiveness and efficiency of the training function. This project on "**Evaluation of Training for Duties of DDOs in Taxation Matters**"; is specifically undertaken to realize the potential of proper evaluation of the course in improving the effectiveness and efficiency of training function at the training organization.

Levels to incorporate EoT

In order to evaluate the training, it is required to examine the quality of learning activities used for the course participants. In the course, the following issues are identified requiring change to improve the overall evaluation of training:

L

evel -1 (at Reaction level): It is must to examine the quality of learning activities, on which basis it becomes possible to prove the change in behavior (in terms of knowledge, skills, and attitude) of the participants. Since the course DDTM only relies upon the initial expectations of the participants for recording their reactions towards the course, which is not sufficient.

It is required to develop IRQs on which basis the initial and ending behavior can be recorded in terms of their reactions with regard to key training inputs. The IRQs can be analyzed by the training institute for internal validation purposes and by Department of Higher Education and DoPT for external validation purposes. Further, the individual interviews should be used as a tool to record their level of knowledge and skills three times i.e. at starting of the course, mid of the course, and at end of the course for analyzing their learning.

Level -2 (at Learning Outcomes): The course DDTM states the following objectives to be achieved:

- Describe the provisions of Income Tax with latest amendments
- Compute Income Tax as per latest amended rules for the Financial Year 2018-19 for ensuring accurate deduction of tax at source

- Submit e-TDS return (24Q) as per Government Instructions
- Describe the provisions of Goods and Services Tax particularly with emphasis upon duties of Drawing and Disbursing Officers (DDOs)

In order to measure the learning outcomes, an objective test should be developed at the end of the course to check and verify the learning of the participants. A questionnaire should also be constructed comprises exercises to compute the accurate amount of tax deduction at source (TDS) as per rules of income tax act. In order to check the learning on provisions of Goods and Service Tax, a role play exercise can be developed which can be performed on the 2nd day of the course. The records relating to responses of the participants, on objective tests, questionnaires should be maintained in the final report of the course.

Level -3 (at Job Performance): At present, there is no mechanism to check the job performance of the participants at DHE.

They participate in the course and thereafter starting performing their functions in their offices and the DHE does not use any type of verification with regard to change in behavior (knowledge, skills, and attitude) before and after the training. It is required to frame various simulation and in-tray exercises keeping in view the situations of concerned client organizations. For example, in case of DDTM course, simulation and in-tray exercises should be framed comprising the tasks of ensuring comp The client organization should use that exercise to verify the learning of the participants and also involve the participant similar tasks at the workspace for at least one month so that their skills can be sharpen at their jobs. The level of skills should be maintained in the learning logs at the client level so that each employee is selected for the next training on the basis of their learning logs.

Level -4 (at **Results Achieved**): The course DDTM was organized to enhance the capabilities of the participants with regard to accurate deduction of tax, submission of e-TDS, and implementation of Goods and Service Tax at their workspace.

Whether the results have been achieved in the form of their enriched learning in this regard that should be checked by DHE and record in the learning logs of the participants with a copy to the training organization and DoPT.

Deficiencies identified in EoT function of the training organization

For each training programme, the evaluation system is weak in terms of measurement of performance of trainee at their workspace. There is no system to assess the performance at the ground level. After imparting training, whether the trainees are performing more effectively or not; that is missing on part of evaluation of training. Further, the funding agencies are being provided reports on the course components by the training organization. As far as evaluation of results achieved is concerned, neither the funding agencies nor the client organizations adopt a robust evaluation system. It is required to improve the overall effectiveness of EoT function at the training organization.

Aims of the Project

The main aim of this project is devise a better EoT system for evaluating training courses by using various tools including learning logs, developing more objective type tests & constructing questionnaires for the participants, use of group exercises and role plays during the course, use of simulations and individual interviews for internal and external validation of the participants, behavior analysis, better evaluation of feedback, stakeholders' analysis, responsibility mapping, EoT matrix etc. The project is also aimed to measure the effectiveness and efficiency of the course in terms of performance of the participants at their workspace in the client organization and to make available adequate information for funding organizations like Department of Personnel and Training, in the evaluation report of a course.

Methodology of the Project

In order to achieve the aims of the project, various tasks of evaluating the training function will be identified and steps will be recommended to incorporate the tools of EoT. The key stakeholders i.e. DDOs, Director General of the training organization, Director General of DHE, and Head of DoPT will be provided adequate information to evaluate the effectiveness and efficiency of DDTM course in improving the behavior of the DDOs. On the basis of information of the course, the learning logs of the DDOs will be maintained at both organizations i.e. the training organization and DHE. On the basis of job performance of DDOs and achievement of key objectives of the training, further training needs will be identified by the training organization and DHE.

Key Tasks for EoT

In order to improve the EoT function, the following tools of EoT can be used:

(i)   Using Learning Logs:

It is well known that the level of learning differs from one person to another and during training, if the level of learning of the participants is not much different, then it becomes easier for the training organization to realize the goals of training effectively. The participants' learning will be assessed in the following format, during the training by the Course Director:

<table>
<tr><td>

- Name of Participant:

- Date:

- Learning Event (i.e. Training input):

- What the participant learned during the sessions:

- How the learning can be applied at workspace?

- When the learning can be applied at workspace?

- Action planned by the participant

- Potential opportunities for further professional development

</td></tr>
</table>

The learning logs will be assessed by the Course Director and will be a part of the Course Director's report, to keep in the training records of the training organization. A copy of the report will be sent to the DHE, for maintaining record of the participants' learning. In case of DDTM, the learning log of each participant may be the following:

<table>
<tr><td>

- Name of Participant: ____________________

- Date: ____________________

</td></tr>
</table>

> • Learning Event (i.e. Training input): Duties of DDOs in Taxation Matters (DDTM) at the training organization
>
> • What the participant learned during the sessions: Accurate deduction of TDS, Submission of e-TDS, and Implementation of GST
>
> • How the learning can be applied at workspace: In financial transactions relating to employees and contractors' payment; the participant can compute the accurate amount of TDS and GST applicable in the provided transaction. He can also submit the e-TDS return at the end of each quarter.
>
> • When the learning can be applied at workspace: Whenever financial transactions relating to employees and contractors' payment happen in his office.
>
> • Action planned by the participant: The participant will himself compute the amount of TDS and GST in all financial transactions.
>
> • Potential opportunities for further professional development: The participant expressed interest to further develop his taxation skills by participating in another programme related to Goods and Services Tax (GST).

(ii)   Developing Objective Type Tests

During the course, the trainers and course directors formally assessed the knowledge and skills of the participants. It is required to develop objective type tests for each course at the training organization which can be used during the training programme for better assessment of the participants. In DDTM course, the short answer items can be developed by the trainer or guest faculty invited to deliver sessions on income tax. The short answer items can be used every time in DDTM course. For example:

1. What is the first thing you must do if the 24Q (e-TDS) is not submitted on the due date?

   ____
   ____
   ____
   ____
   ____

2. If an employee's net tax liability is Rs. 5,00,000 then how much TDS will you deduct from his monthly salary:

   ____
   ____

The objective type test may also include the multiple choice items presenting the practical problems at workspace with the several alternatives to the solutions. The participant may be asked to select the most appropriate solution. In case of DDTM course, the following multiple choice items can be included in the test:

The house rent allowance will become fully taxable if

(a) The employee has not submitted the certificate of rent payment

(b) The employee's taxable salary is more than 5,00,000

(c) The employee has given his consent to deduct tax on house rent allowance

(d) The taxable income becomes more than basic exemption limit and employee is not paying any rent

In the above multi-choice item, the answer will be (d). In order to check the learning of the training session on income tax, the above multi-choice item can be used to test the participants.

(iii)   Constructing Questionnaires

In order to validate the learning through the training of DDTM course, the subject experts will construct a questionnaire for the DDOs. First of all, a suitable questionnaire will be framed and constructed by writing the questions (in form of Checklists and Multiple Choice Questions) to seek the information upon the learning from the course. Thereafter, the questionnaire will be distributed among the DDOs at appropriate time during the training. The course director will record, analysis, and interpret the results of the responses provided to the questionnaire by using MS-Excel spreadsheets.

(iv)   Behavior Analysis

In order to analyze the behavior of participants, groups should be constituted in each course. The participants behave in differently while working in the constituted groups. The course director and faculties should analyze the behavior of each participant during the course at the time of group interactions. The DDOs usually become angry with the employees for deducting the tax and sometimes, the conflicts are also take place for long term in the colleges. It is must to sharpen their social skills by equip them with the task of behavior analysis. The participants will be provided a role-play exercise containing 3 roles i.e. DDO, employee, and observer. The DDO will be provided task to deduct accurate amount of tax while the employee will be provided task to convince DDO not to deduct accurate amount of tax due to his weak financial situation. The observer will note down the behavior of both in terms of proposing, giving information, supporting, building, seeking information, summarizing, disagreeing, bringing in, shutting out, defending, and testing. The behavior analysis will be noted down by the observer. Thereafter in another round, the roles will be changed and 2nd case will be distributed relating to 3 roles i.e. DDO, Contractor, and Observer. Since the roles are changed, the observers will note down the behavior on the same parameters as in 1st round. Similarly, in 3rd round, 3rd case will be distributed relating to 3 roles i.e. DDO, Auditor, and Observer. The behavior of each participant will be observed and noted down and keep in record with the course director. The training organization, can utilize the behavior analysis on the basis of role-play exercises and the involvement of the participants to decide their behavior in the situations relating to taxation matters.

(v)   EoT Matrix:

As per EoT matrix, the training can be evaluated at four levels i.e. Reaction level, Learning Outcomes, Job Performance, and Results Achieved. There may be four purposes of evaluation on these four levels i.e. to check learning process of the participants, proving their learning & development, improving their learning by interventions, and monitoring their learning and development. The training organization for the course DDTM can seek the information firstly from the participants on the IRQ at the starting & closing of the course to record their reactions. Further, at the end of the course i.e. the learning outcomes level, the training organization can seek information relating to learning from the course and how the learning can be applied at their workspace (using learning logs). Further, the Department of Higher Education after the completion of training may provide the charge of checking and verifying the accurate amount of tax being deducting in various colleges and then give their report in written to the department. The job performance can be checked with regard to the learning in the DDTM course. The information upon the job performance of each participant will be disseminated to the training organization and DoPT. Further, on the basis of information received from participants (in form of IRQs), from the training organization (in form of Course Director's Report & comments of Director General), from DHE (in form of job performance of each participant); the EoT Matrix can be developed by the training organization, DHE, and DoPT for each participant to decide further their training needs. The process of EoT matrix will continuously help each stakeholder to raise the level of performance of the participants.

Stakeholder Analysis:

In DDTM course, the DDOs, Course Director, Director General of the training organization, Director General of DHE, and Head of DoPT are the stakeholders. The following issues are identified and views of stakeholders are also provided:

Stakeholders' names	
	DDOs – D
	Course Director – CD
	Director General – DG
	Director General of DHE – DG_DHE
	Head of DoPT – H_DoPT

Keys:

Indicators	
	+ means Support
	- means Oppose
	o means neutral
	? means uncertain

The views are expressed as under:

Change / Issues	Stakeholders Analysis				
	D	CD	DG	DG_DHE	H_DoPT
1. Introduce and use of Learning Logs for imparting training and evaluating participants	+	+	+	+	+
2. Introduce and use of Objective Type Tests	-	+	+	-	0
3. Construction of questionnaires and interpreting for evaluating results	-	+	+	-	0
4. Involve DHE in maintaining records of EoT	?	+	+	-	+
5. Propose cost / benefit analysis	+	-	-	+	+

On the basis of analysis, it seems that the learning logs are possible to be introduced and used without any resistance to change in the stakeholders.

However, in case of Objective type tests & questionnaires for evaluating training function in DDOs, the DDOs are opposing to be tested in the training and even their department i.e. DHE is also opposing, this change can take place only after convincing them and the training organization can arrange a meeting for the same. The DHE is also opposing for the maintenance of records relating to evaluation and in this regard, DoPT can issue the directions to DHE for maintenance of the records for ensuring learning and development activities. The cost benefit analysis can be introduced after convincing the training organization for undertaking this work. The DHE and DoPT can also do cost-benefit analysis even after resistance from the training organization.

Mapping Responsibilities

The main aim of this project is devise a better EoT system for evaluating training courses by using various tools including learning logs, developing more objective type tests & constructing questionnaires for the participants, use of group exercises and role plays during the course, use of simulations and individual interviews for internal and external validation of the participants, behavior analysis, better evaluation of feedback, stakeholders' analysis, responsibility mapping, EoT matrix etc. The project is also aimed to measure the effectiveness and efficiency of the course in terms of performance of the participants at their workspace in the client organization and to make available adequate information for funding organizations like Department of Personnel and Training, in the evaluation report of a course. It is required to play various roles by different people to implement the EoT change:

Director General of the training organization	- Prepare Standard Operating Procedure (SoP) for Evaluation of Training by incorporating learning logs, objective type tests and questionnaire's use in each course - Incorporate internal audit team to monitor the progress of EoT function as per SoP - A separate wing in training branch to analyze the assessments of courses in terms of effectiveness and efficiency of training function
Head of Client Organizations	- Preparation of Learning logs of each employee and assess change in behavior (i.e. knowledge, skills, and attitude) - Identification of suitable trainees for each training course - External Validation of trainees after participating in a course - Reports on the job performance of each employee including SWOT Analysis
Trainees	- Building learning log and expressing the

	interest to participate in an appropriate course as per SWOT Analysis - Practice the learning from the course and submit the report to DHE and the training organization
Funding Agencies	- External validation of the course by qualitative assessments using EoT tools mentioned in the report - Regular intervention in the training function to improve the EoT function - Checks and granting funds on the basis of achievement of job performance and key results

Implementation Details

The implementation of change in an organization is one of the difficult tasks and it requires firm determination and strategies to incorporate the change. The following steps can be taken for improving the EoT function at the training organization:

i. For each course, like DDTM, it is required to prepare the learning logs and maintain the records

ii.   Preparation of objective type tests and questionnaires for each course and convincing trainees as well as client organization to accept the use of tests and questionnaires in courses

iii.   Development of psychometric tests for measurement of behavior of the participants and analyzing their learning from the training and development activities

iv.   Preparation of EoT matrix for each course and proper evaluation of each participant on the basis of the matrix. The decisions of providing training again if external validation proves that there is no significant improvement in behavior (in terms of knowledge, skills, and attitude) after the training course

v.   Fixing the responsibilities of the authorities to monitor, evaluation and identify further training needs of the participants (or employees).

Action Plan:

The following steps will be taken to implement the change in the existing system:

- **Learning logs**
  - Prepartation of learning logs by Course Directors and Head of Client Organization
  - SWOT Analysis of the employees with regard to job performance

- **Ojective type tests**
  - Preparing Objective Type Tests for use during the course by Resource Persons
  - Making provisions for incorporating objective type tests by Director General of HIPA

- **Questionnaires**
  - Contruction of questionnaires by the subject experts on each training input
  - Ensuring the use of each questionnaire in related training inputs by Course Director

- **Behaviour**
  - Use of Behaviour Analysis exercises at the starting and end of the course
  - Assessment of change in behaviour at the time of job performance

- **EoT matrix**
  - Manipulating EoT matrix of each course for each participant by the Course Director
  - According to EoT matrix, taking the decision on training needs, learnings, assessment of the participants

Anticipation of Further Changes:

The EoT function should be improved by using software, websites, and applets. More the use of information technology, more accurate results will be there for assessing the performance, needs, and achievement of key objectives. A suitable system should be there to internal audit the processes of the EoT function and as per requirement, the process restructuring should be used to modify the overall EoT function in order to improve the effectiveness and efficiency of the training function of the training organization.

Benefits

There are multi-fold benefits from the project in improving the EoT function:

Benefits to the Training Organization:

1) Maintenance of learning logs of the participants already trained in the organization and accurate training needs analysis

2) Improvement in the effectiveness of formative and summative assessments of the courses by using immediate response questionnaires, objective type tests and multiple choice questions

3) Up-gradation of quality of the training by adding value to the EoT function leading to overall improvement

4) Fixation of responsibilities of the stakeholders on part of training organization

Benefits to the Participants:

1) Boosting confidence of the participating by imparting training of more effectiveness

2) Accurate assessment of the training function through behavior analysis (KSA Approach) improves the strengths of the participants

3) Employee's value in terms of skills will increase after training and he will be recognized as more valuable assets to the client organization

4) Development of a sense of empowerment through right evaluation

5) Promotion can easily be realized by adding the skills and improving the attitude at job performance

Benefits to the Client Organizations:

1) The EoT function's implementation will formulate the database of learning logs of each employee and the right work can be given to the right person.

2) The delegation of authority can be possible and effective decentralization of authority will improve the overall performance of the organization

3) The waste of resource will be minimized to a great extent and the efficiency will improve in each function of the organization

4) The conductive environment for the employee through proper training will improve the job satisfaction level in the organization which has further various benefits

Benefit to the Funding Agencies:

1) With the same cost of training, the benefits to the client organization will be increased, overall benefit in achievement of objectives of the course.

2) The funding agencies can justify the performance of training in terms of the cost-benefit analysis

3) The EoT function will support the funding agencies to compare & select the right organizations to impart training

EXECUTIVE SUMMARY

The project on which basis, the book is formulated was **"Evaluation of Training for Duties of DDOs in Taxation Matters"**, organized at a training institution. At present, various parameters of training progress and non-training interventions' performance are assessed for the training courses organized at the training organization. The responses of participants received as summative assessment, are analyzed using measures of central tendency, measures of variations, and cross tabulation analysis of the data in MS-Excel software; to determine the necessary corrective measures for improving the effectiveness and efficiency of the training function. In this EoT project, a course of DDTM is taken under consideration to explain the system of evaluation at the training organization. The course was firstly inaugurated by the Director General on the first day (in first session). Thereafter, the Course Director assessed the initial reactions and expectations of the participants. The participants were asked to explain their expectations from the course so that the course design may be modified (if required). In the course DDTM, after getting the initial reactions and responses with regard to the expectations from the course, various exercises on Goods and Service Tax (GST) had been added containing understanding of practical issues.

The DDTM course is organized for the Director General, Department of Higher Education (DHE); to train their employees i.e. college principals who require to ensure compliance of provisions relating to taxation (including income tax and goods & services tax) in the transactions of colleges. The college principals are designated as Drawing and Disbursing Officer (DDO) for making financial transactions and ensuring compliance of financial rules including taxation in the colleges. Since the DDOs are responsible to compliance the provisions of income tax, value added tax, goods and services tax, apart from their duties with regard to drawing and disburse accurate amount in making expenditures at their workplace and due to their large involvement in administrative functions, they suffered from lack of time to deal the work of DDO. For the course of DDTM, the objectives have been stated as under:

By the end of this course participants should be able to:

- Describe the provisions of Income Tax with latest amendments
- Compute Income Tax as per latest amended rules for the Financial Year 2018–19 for ensuring accurate deduction of tax at source
- Submit e-TDS return (24Q) as per Government Instructions
- Describe the provisions of Goods and Services Tax particularly with emphasis upon duties of Drawing and Disbursing Officers (DDOs)

Keeping in view the above stated objectives, the training design has been prepared and sent to the DHE. The course has been organized at the training organization and at the end of the quality, quantity; relevance and utility of the training inputs as well as non-training interventions have been evaluated through an evaluation questionnaire provided to the participants for giving their responses on various parameters. At the end of the course, during valedictory address, the participants have also been asked to give their views including remarks on shortcomings of training function, non-training interventions etc.; so that accordingly the improvements can be decided to took place for strengthening the training function of the organization. The evaluation questionnaire used to evaluate the responses of participants of the course "Duties of DDOs in Taxation Matters" is enclosed as Annexure – "A". On the basis of responses of the participants, a Course Director Report (CDR) is prepared by the Course Director and submitted to the Director General of the training organization (enclosed as Annexure – "B"). The CDR with remarks of the Director General is sent to the funding organization i.e. Department of Personnel and Training (DoPT). The information relating to number of participants, their involvement in training, attendance record, and remarks of Course Director; is also sent to the DHE.

The EoT function can be strengthen at the training organization, for improving the effectiveness and efficiency of the training function of the training organization. At present, the client organizations like DHE are not much aware of contribution of the training organization in developing the human resources and this project focuses on recommending the change in EoT function for prepare and provide information relating to training and development of each participant, on which basis the client organizations can further decide to improve the effectiveness and efficiencies of the employees. It is required to improve the EoT function to have more effective external validation by the client organizations and funding organizations including DoPT. The client organizations and funding organization on the basis of evaluation report will be able to prepare cost-benefit analysis of the course to justify the relevance of training at the training organization.

L evels to incorporate EoT :

In order to evaluate the training, it is required to examine the quality of learning activities used for the course participants. In the course, the following issues are identified requiring change to improve the overall evaluation of training:

(a) **Level -1 (at Reaction level):** It is must to examine the quality of learning activities, on which basis it becomes possible to prove the change in behavior (in terms of knowledge, skills, and attitude) of the participants. Since the course DDTM only relies upon the initial expectations of the participants for recording their reactions towards the course, which is not sufficient. It is required to develop IRQs on which basis the initial and ending behavior can be recorded in terms of their reactions with regard to key training inputs. The IRQs can be analyzed by the training institute for internal validation purposes and by Department of Higher Education and DoPT for external validation purposes. Further, the individual interviews should be used as a tool to record their level of knowledge and skills three times i.e. at starting of the course, mid of the course, and at end of the course for analyzing their learning.

(b) **Level -2 (at Learning Outcomes):** The course DDTM states the following objectives to be achieved:

- Describe the provisions of Income Tax with latest amendments
- Compute Income Tax as per latest amended rules for the Financial Year 2018-19 for ensuring accurate deduction of tax at source
- Submit e-TDS return (24Q) as per Government Instructions
- Describe the provisions of Goods and Services Tax particularly with emphasis upon duties of Drawing and Disbursing Officers (DDOs)

In order to measure the learning outcomes, an objective test should be developed at the end of the course to check and verify the learning of the participants. A questionnaire should also be constructed comprises exercises to compute the accurate amount of tax deduction at source (TDS) as per rules of income tax act. In order to check the learning on provisions of Goods and Service Tax, a role play exercise can be developed which can be performed on the 2nd day of the course. The records relating to responses of the participants, on objective tests, questionnaires should be maintained in the final report of the course.

(c) **Level -3 (at Job Performance):** At present, there is no mechanism to check the job performance of the participants at DHE. They participate in the course and thereafter starting performing their functions in their offices and the DHE does not use any type of verification with regard to change in behavior (knowledge, skills, and attitude) before and after the training. It is required to frame various simulation and in-tray exercises keeping in view the situations of concerned client organizations. For example, in case of DDTM course, simulation and in-tray exercises should be framed comprising the tasks of ensuring comp The client organization should use that exercise to verify the learning of the participants and also involve the participant similar tasks at the workspace for at least one month so that their skills can be sharpen at their jobs. The level of skills should be maintained in the learning logs at the client level so that each employee is selected for the next training on the basis of their learning logs.

(d) **Level -4 (at Results Achieved):** The course DDTM was organized to enhance the capabilities of the participants with regard to accurate deduction of tax, submission of e-TDS, and implementation of Goods and Service Tax at their workspace. Whether the results have been achieved in the form of their enriched learning in this regard that should be checked by DHE and record in the learning logs of the participants with a copy to the training organization and DoPT.

Deficiencies identified in EoT function of the training organization: For each training programme, the evaluation system is weak in terms of measurement of performance of trainee at their workspace. There is no system to assess the performance at the ground level. After imparting training, whether the trainees are performing more effectively or not; that is missing on part of evaluation of training. Further, the funding agencies are being provided reports on the course components by the training organization. As far as evaluation of results achieved is concerned, neither the funding agencies nor the client organizations adopt a robust evaluation system. It is required to improve the overall effectiveness of EoT function at the training organization.

Aims of the Project:

The main aim of this project is devise a better EoT system for evaluating training courses by using various tools including learning logs, developing more objective type tests & constructing questionnaires for the participants, use of group exercises and role plays during the course, use of simulations and individual interviews for internal and external validation of the participants, behavior analysis, better evaluation of feedback, stakeholders' analysis, responsibility mapping, EoT matrix etc. The project is also aimed to measure the effectiveness and efficiency of the course in terms of performance of the participants at their workspace in the client organization and to make available adequate information for funding organizations like Department of Personnel and Training, in the evaluation report of a course.

Methodology of the Project:

In order to achieve the aims of the project, various tasks of evaluating the training function will be identified and steps will be recommended to incorporate the tools of EoT. The key stakeholders i.e. DDOs, Director General of the training organization, Director General of DHE, and Head of DoPT will be provided adequate information to evaluate the effectiveness and efficiency of DDTM course in improving the behavior of the DDOs. On the basis of information of the course, the learning logs of the DDOs will be maintained at both organizations the training organization and DHE. On the basis of job performance of DDOs and achievement of key objectives of the training, further training needs will be identified by the training organization and DHE.

Key Tasks for EoT:

In order to improve the EoT function, the following tools of EoT can be used:

1. **Using Learning Logs:**

It is well known that the level of learning differs from one person to another and during training, if the level of learning of the participants is not much different, then it becomes easier for the training organization to realize the goals of training effectively. The participants' learning will be assessed in the following format, during the training by the Course Director:

> - Name of Participant:
>
> - Date:
>
> - Learning Event (i.e. Training input):
>
> - What the participant learned during the sessions:
>
> - How the learning can be applied at workspace?
>
> - When the learning can be applied at workspace?
>
> - Action planned by the participant
>
> - Potential opportunities for further professional development

The learning logs will be assessed by the Course Director and will be a part of the Course Director's report, to keep in the training records of the training organization. A copy of the report will be sent to the DHE, for maintaining record of the participants' learning. In case of DDTM, the learning log of each participant may be the following:

> - Name of Participant: ___________________
>
> - Date: ___________________
>
> - Learning Event (i.e. Training input): Duties of DDOs in Taxation Matters (DDTM) at the training organization
>
> - What the participant learned during the sessions: Accurate deduction of TDS, Submission of e-TDS, and Implementation of GST
>
> - How the learning can be applied at workspace: In financial

transactions relating to employees and contractors' payment; the participant can compute the accurate amount of TDS and GST applicable in the provided transaction. He can also submit the e-TDS return at the end of each quarter.

• When the learning can be applied at workspace: Whenever financial transactions relating to employees and contractors' payment happen in his office.

• Action planned by the participant: The participant will himself compute the amount of TDS and GST in all financial transactions.

• Potential opportunities for further professional development: The participant expressed interest to further develop his taxation skills by participating in another programme related to Goods and Services Tax (GST).

2. **Developing Objective Type Tests**

During the course, the trainers and course directors formally assessed the knowledge and skills of the participants. It is required to develop objective type tests for each course at the training organization which can be used during the training programme for better assessment of the participants. In DDTM course, the short answer items can be developed by the trainer or guest faculty invited to deliver sessions on income tax. The short answer items can be used every time in DDTM course. For example:

3. What is the first thing you must do if the 24Q (e–TDS) is not submitted on the due date?

____

____

____

____

____

4. If an employee's net tax liability is Rs. 5,00,000 then how much TDS will you deduct from his monthly salary:

____

____

The objective type test may also include the multiple choice items presenting the practical problems at workspace with the several alternatives to the solutions. The participant may be asked to select the most appropriate solution. In case of DDTM course, the following multiple choice items can be included in the test:

The house rent allowance will become fully taxable if

(e) The employee has not submitted the certificate of rent payment

(f) The employee's taxable salary is more than 5,00,000

(g) The employee has given his consent to deduct tax on house rent allowance

(h) The taxable income becomes more than basic exemption limit and employee is not paying any rent

In the above multi-choice item, the answer will be (d). In order to check the learning of the training session on income tax, the above multi-choice item can be used to test the participants.

3. Constructing Questionnaires

In order to validate the learning through the training of DDTM course, the subject experts will construct a questionnaire for the DDOs. First of all, a suitable questionnaire will be framed and constructed by writing the questions (in form of Checklists and Multiple Choice Questions) to seek the information upon the learning from the course. Thereafter, the questionnaire will be distributed among the DDOs at appropriate time during the training. The course director will record, analysis, and interpret the results of the responses provided to the questionnaire by using MS-Excel spreadsheets.

4. Behavior Analysis

In order to analyze the behavior of participants, groups should be constituted in each course. The participants behave in differently while working in the constituted groups. The course director and faculties should analyze the behavior of each participant during the course at the time of group interactions. The DDOs usually become angry with the employees for deducting the tax and sometimes, the conflicts are also take place for long term in the colleges. It is must to sharpen their social skills by equip them with the task of behavior analysis. The participants will be provided a role-play exercise containing 3 roles i.e. DDO, employee, and observer. The DDO will be provided task to deduct accurate amount of tax while the employee will be provided task to convince DDO not to deduct accurate amount of tax due to his weak financial situation. The observer will note down the behavior of both in terms of proposing, giving information, supporting, building, seeking information, summarizing, disagreeing, bringing in, shutting out, defending, and testing. The behavior analysis will be noted down by the observer. Thereafter in another round, the roles will be changed and 2nd case will be distributed relating to 3 roles i.e. DDO, Contractor, and Observer. Since the roles are changed, the observers will note down the behavior on the same parameters as in 1st round. Similarly, in 3rd round, 3rd case will be distributed relating to 3 roles i.e. DDO, Auditor, and Observer. The behavior of each participant will be observed and noted down and keep in record with the course director. The training organization, can utilize the behavior analysis on the basis of role-play exercises and the involvement of the participants to decide their behavior in the situations relating to taxation matters.

5. **EoT Matrix:**

As per EoT matrix, the training can be evaluated at four levels i.e. Reaction level, Learning Outcomes, Job Performance, and Results Achieved. There may be four purposes of evaluation on these four levels i.e. to check learning process of the participants, proving their learning & development, improving their learning by interventions, and monitoring their learning and development. The training organization for the course DDTM can seek the information firstly from the participants on the IRQ at the starting & closing of the course to record their reactions. Further, at the end of the course i.e. the learning outcomes level, the training organization can seek information relating to learning from the course and how the learning can be applied at their workspace (using learning logs). Further, the Department of Higher Education after the completion of training may provide the charge of checking and verifying the accurate amount of tax being deducting in various colleges and then give their report in written to the department. The job performance can be checked with regard to the learning in the DDTM course. The information upon the job performance of each participant will be disseminated to the training organization and DoPT. Further, on the basis of information received from participants (in form of IRQs), from the training organization (in form of Course Director's Report & comments of Director General of the training organization), from DHE (in form of job performance of each participant); the EoT Matrix can be developed by the training organization, DHE, and DoPT for each participant to decide further their training needs. The process of EoT matrix will continuously help each stakeholder to raise the level of performance of the participants.

6. **Stakeholder Analysis:**

In DDTM course, the DDOs, Course Director, Director General of the training organization, Director General of DHE, and Head of DoPT are the stakeholders. The following issues are identified and views of stakeholders are also provided:

Stakeholders' names	DDOs – D
	Course Director – CD
	Director General – DG
	Director General of DHE – DG_DHE
	Head of DoPT – H_DoPT

Keys:

Indicators	+ means Support
	- means Oppose
	0 means neutral
	? means uncertain

The views are expressed as under:

Change / Issues	Stakeholders Analysis				
	D	CD	DG	DG_DHE	H_DoPT
• Introduce and use of Learning Logs for imparting training and evaluating participants	+	+	+	+	+
• Introduce and use of Objective Type Tests	–	+	+	–	0
• Construction of	–	+	+	–	0

questionnaires and interpreting for evaluating results					
• Involve DHE in maintaining records of EoT	?	+	+	−	+
• Propose cost / benefit analysis	+	−	−	+	+

On the basis of analysis, it seems that the learning logs are possible to be introduced and used without any resistance to change in the stakeholders. However, in case of Objective type tests & questionnaires for evaluating training function in DDOs, the DDOs are opposing to be tested in the training and even their department i.e. DHE is also opposing, this change can take place only after convincing them and the training organization can arrange a meeting for the same. The DHE is also opposing for the maintenance of records relating to evaluation and in this regard, DoPT can issue the directions to DHE for maintenance of the records for ensuring learning and development activities. The cost benefit analysis can be introduced after convincing the training organization for undertaking this work. The DHE and DoPT can also do cost-benefit analysis even after resistance from the training organization.

The main aim of this project is devise a better EoT system for evaluating training courses by using various tools including learning logs, developing more objective type tests & constructing questionnaires for the participants, use of group exercises and role plays during the course, use of simulations and individual interviews for internal and external validation of the participants, behavior analysis, better evaluation of feedback, stakeholders' analysis, responsibility mapping, EoT matrix etc.

Implementation of Change in EoT function:

The implementation of change in an organization is one of the difficult tasks and it requires firm determination and strategies to incorporate the change. The following steps can be taken for improving the EoT function at the training organization:

1. For each course, like DDTM, it is required to prepare the learning logs and maintain the records

2. Preparation of objective type tests and questionnaires for each course and convincing trainees as well as client organization to accept the use of tests and questionnaires in courses

3. Development of psychometric tests for measurement of behavior of the participants and analyzing their learning from the training and development activities

4.   Preparation of EoT matrix for each course and proper evaluation of each participant on the basis of the matrix. The decisions of providing training again if external validation proves that there is no significant improvement in behavior (in terms of knowledge, skills, and attitude) after the training course

5.   Fixing the responsibilities of the authorities to monitor, evaluation and identify further training needs of the participants (or employees).

Action Plan:

The following steps will be taken to implement the change in the existing system:

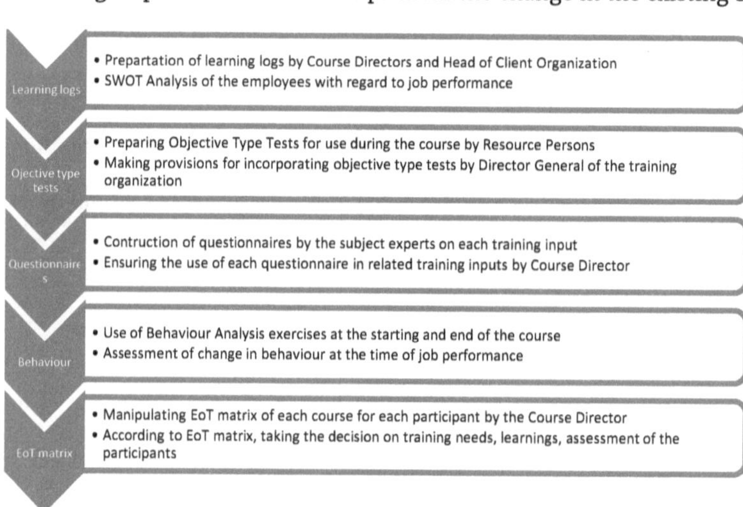

–ANNEXURE – "A"

COURSE EVALUATION QUESTIONNAIRE

**(Note: Please fill in the items in the questionnaire. Your objectivity
will help us to improve the future Course)**

1. Name of the Institution   :
2. Title of the Training: Course on **"Duties of DDOs in Taxation Matters (Income Tax and Goods and Services Tax)" (Sponsored by DoPT, Govt. of India)**
3. Date conducted   :
4. Course Director   :

5.Course Objectives:

By the end of this course participants should be able to:

• Describe the provisions of Income Tax with latest amendments

• Compute Income Tax as per latest amended rules for the Financial Year 2018-19

for ensuring accurate deduction of tax at source

• Submit e-TDS return (24Q) as per Government Instructions

• Describe the provisions of Goods and Services Tax particularly with emphasis upon duties of Drawing and Disbursing Officers (DDOs)

1. Did you receive advance intimation from the Institution about the programme? If so, did you respond to the Institution?

YES   NO

7.   What do you think about the structure and organization of the Course to meet the objectives?

Very well Structured	Well Structured	Some–what Un–structured	Very Un–structured
4	3	2	1

8. How useful this training be to you immediately in your job?

Very Useful	Quite Useful	Of limited use	Not at all Useful
4	3	2	1

9. How useful this training likely to be for the future jobs you may handle?

Very useful	Quite useful	Of limited use	Not at all Useful
4	3	2	1

10. Practical orientation of the Course:

Highly Practical	Practically Oriented to a Great extent	Practically Oriented to a Limited extent	Not at all Practically Oriented
4	3	2	1

11. How far have you been benefited from interaction with the fellow participants during the Course?

Substantially	Considerably	Fairly	Not at all
4	3	2	1

12. How far was the Course material supplied relevant and related to the Course content?

Extremely Relevant	Considerably Relevant	Fairly relevant	Not at all relevant
4	3	2	1

13. To what extent are you satisfied with the following:

(The Institution should delete the rows, which are not applicable)

	Satisfied fully	Satisfied to a large extent	Satisfied to a limited extent	Not satisfied at all
	4	3	2	1
a) Reception & Transport				
b) Residential Accommodation				
c) Food Quality And Service				
d) Class room Facilities				
e) Library				

Facilities				
f) Computer Facilities				
g) Interaction with The Faculty				

14. Assessment of training Faculty:

	Session Duration	Topics	Faculty name internal / external	Assessment			
				Exce llent	Very Good	Good	Fair
				4	3	2	1
	Monday	Registration					
	9:30 AM –10:45 AM	Inaugural address and Introduction to the Course					
	11:00 AM –12:15 PM	An overview to Income Tax Computation for Salaried Persons					
	2:00 PM – 3:15 PM	Deductions and Exemptions in Income Tax Act					
	Tuesday 9:30 AM –10:45 AM	Submission of e-TDS return (24Q)					
	11:00 AM –12:15 PM	Implementation of GST in Government Organizations & Duties of DDOs & Head of Government					

		Offices					
	12:15 PM -3:15 PM	An exercise on computation of TDS for F.Y. 2018-19					
	Wednesday 9:30 AM -10:45 AM	e-Filing Income Tax Return					
	11:00 AM -1:30 PM	Group Presentations on problems related to Income Tax & GST in Government Offices					
	2:00 PM - 3:15 PM	Feedback and Valedictory Address					

15.   Which parts of the Course did you find most helpful?

16.   Which parts of the Course did you find least helpful?

17.   Your overall impression of the Course:

Excellent	Very Good	Good	Fair
4	3	2	1

18.   Did the Course give you any specific ideas about improvements in your working situation when you get back:

YES/NO

19.   If yes, can you spell them out briefly?

20.   Any other comments/observations you wish to make about the Course.

Dated: **Name :**
                                                  Designation:
                                                  Organization

-ANNEXURE – "B"

COURSE DIRECTOR's REPORT

1. Name of the :
   Institution

2. Title of the Course : "Duties of DDOs in Taxation Matters (Income Tax and Goods and Services Tax)" (**Sponsored by DoPT, Govt. of India**)

3. Duration of the Course :

4. Course Team :

   :

5. No. of Participants: : (List attached at annexure 'A')
   (Please enclose a copy of the final list of participants duly classified).

6.	Number of those who submitted feedback form:	:	
	(a)Whether the Institution got in touch in advance with the participants of the course		Yes
			Letters have been written one month before organizing course.
	(b) If so, when; and		
	(c)How many participants responded?		
7.	Whether the course expectations of the participants were ascertained by the Institution if so how and when?	:	The expectations of the participants are asked on the very first day at the time of introducing the course. A brief introduction on each component of the programme is provided and asked whether there is any requirement to add or reduce something from that component.

8. General observations : of the Course Director on how the course was organised:

Please indicate:

| a) Whether the course was conducted at the Institution's campus or elsewhere (if so where) | Yes. |

Non-residential.

b) Whether the course was "residential" or "non-residential" (if residential, whether the residential facilities were provided in the Institution's own hostel or in a hotel etc.

Three Days

c)	(1)	Total number of working days in the course

Four Sessions per day (each of 75 minutes)

(2)	Number of working hours per day

Twelve Sessions

(3)	Total number of
sessions planned in the course

None

(4)	Number of sessions
which could not be
conducted as planned:

Please see annexure 'B'

Please see annexure 'C'

(Please enclose a copy of

-	The final

course time-table

- The list of a
faculty (both in house
and guest faculty)

9. General remarks of the Course Director on the nature and extent of participant's involvement in the course, including attendance punctuality, and interest evinced:

The participants remained punctual during all sessions and took keen interest in learning the procedures. On their demand, greater emphasis has been given to New Pension Scheme and GST. The participants asked various practical problems during the sessions and group presentations; the practical solutions to each problem have been provided. The manuals available online on website of income tax department have been shared and interacted. The participants participated very sincerely in each training session. They have showed their interest by noting down each and every learning point in their note books and the soft-copies of each session along with referred notes, have been sent to their e-mail IDs. The course has been proved beneficial as per the feedback of the participants. They rated each training session very beneficial and the practical exercises have also been completed on time.

10.   Comments on the feedback received from participants.:

The whole course has been appreciated by the participants. There was no negative feedback upon the course inputs, faculty, and the quality of food being served to the participants. Overall, the participants delighted from the arrangements of the training programme. The group of 26 officers have been handled by interactions and discussions thoroughly to clear all doubts and group exercises have also been used for in-depth understanding of taxation matters.

11.   Comments of the Institution on how the feedback is proposed to be used for improving future programmes in terms of course content, methodology, etc.:

The training organization generally considers the feedback of the participants in improving the course material, design, and arrangements for the similar courses to be organized in future. Every-time it is tried to take the feedback and comments of the participants, as an improvement to the course activities. The suggestions of the participants will be kept in view while organizing similar course in future. It will be tried to make such programme more application oriented by improving course content, methodology and structure of the course.

12. Any other comments which the Course Director and/or the Institution may wish to make in respect of this course.:

The programme entitled, "Duties of DDOs in Taxation Matters (Income Tax and Goods and Services Tax)" is meant to build and enhance the capacities of officers for strict compliance of taxation rules including income tax and GST. It is required to sensitize the officers for strictly compliance the rules and ensure transparency in tax related operations. The course provides an opportunity to learn and refresh the rules related to taxation. It is must to provide training to the officers at regular intervals so that they become more confident in performing their duties with more sincerity. Next time, it will be tried to fine-tune the structure of course in order to include more topics. The training organization will make it more interactive and easy to understand at the next time, as satisfaction of the participants is the first priority for the institution.

COURSE EVALUATION QUESTIONNAIRE

(Note: Please fill in the items in the questionnaire. Your objectivity will help us to improve the future Course)

1. Name of the Institution   :

2. Title of the Training: Course on **"Duties of DDOs in Taxation Matters (Income Tax and Goods and Services Tax)"** **(Sponsored by DoPT, Govt. of India)**

3. Date conducted   :
4. Course Director   :
5.Course Objectives:

> By the end of this course participants should be able to:
> - Describe the provisions of Income Tax with latest amendments
> - Compute Income Tax as per latest amended rules for the Financial Year 2018-19 for ensuring accurate deduction of tax at source
> - Submit e-TDS return (24Q) as per Government Instructions
> - Describe the provisions of Goods and Services Tax particularly with emphasis upon duties of Drawing and Disbursing Officers (DDOs)

2.Did you receive advance intimation from the Institution about the programme? If so, did you respond to the Institution?

YES ()   **NO ()**

7.What do you think about the structure and organization of the Course   to meet the objectives?

Very well Structured	Well Structured	Some-what *Un-structured*	Very Un-structured	%AGE	Weighted Average
4	3	2	1		

8. How useful this training be to you immediately in your job?

Very Useful	Quite Useful	Of limited use	Not at all Useful	%AGE	Weighted Average
4	3	2	1		

9. How useful this training likely to be for the future jobs you may handle?

Very useful	Quite useful	Of limited use	Not at all Useful	%AGE	Weighted Average
4	3	2	1		

10. Practical orientation of the Course:

Highly Practical	Practically Oriented to a Great extent	Practically Oriented to a Limited extent	Not at all Practically Oriented	%AGE	Weighted Average
4	3	2	1		

11. How far have you been benefited from interaction with the fellow participants during the Course?

Substantially	Considerably	Fairly	Not at all	%AGE	Weighted Average
4	3	2	1		

12. How far was the Course material supplied relevant and related to the Course content?

Extremely Relevant	Considerab ly Relevant	Fairly Relevant	Not at all Relevant	%AGE	W. Average
4	3	2	1		

13. To what extent are you satisfied with the following:
(The Institution should delete the rows, which are not applicable)

	Satisfied Fully	Satisfied to a large extent	Satisfied to a limited extent	Not satisfied at all	Perc enta ge	W. Averag e
	4	3	2	1		
a)Reception and Transport						
b) Food Quality And Service						
c)Class room Facilities						
d) Computer Facilities						
e) Interaction with The Faculty						

14. Assessment of training Faculty:
(Kindly fill up the Table-I of Annexure-V)

15. Which parts of the Course did you find most helpful?

16. Which parts of the Course did you find least helpful?

17. Your overall impression of the Course:

Excellent	Very Good	Good	Fair	%AGE	Weighted Average
4	3	2	1		

18.　　　Did the Course give you any specific ideas about improvements in your working situation when you get back:

YES ()/NO ()

If yes, can you spell them out briefly?

20. Any other comments/observations you wish to make about the Course?

Sr.	Session Duration	Topics	Faculty name internal/ external	Assessment				%	W. Avg
				Excellent	Very Good	Good	Fair		
				4	3	2	1		
1.	**Monday** 9:30 AM – 10:45 AM	Registration							
		Inaugural address and Introduction to the Course							
2.	11:00 AM – 12:15 PM	An overview to Income Tax Computation for Salaried Persons							
3.	2:00 PM – 3:15 PM	Deductions and Exemptions in Income Tax Act							
4.	**Tuesday** 9:30 AM – 10:45 AM	Submission of e-TDS return (24Q)							
5.	11:00 AM – 12:15 PM	Implementation of GST in Government Organizations & Duties of DDOs & Head of Government							

		Offices							
6.	12:15 PM -3:15 PM	An exercise on computation of TDS for F.Y. 2018-19							
10.	**Wednesday** 9:30 AM - 10:45 AM	e-Filing Income Tax Return							
11.	11:00 AM - 1:30 PM	Group Presentations on problems related to Income Tax & GST in Government Offices							
12.	2:00 PM - 3:15 PM	Feedback and Valedictory Address